# THE
# LIGHT FOR
# YOUR PATH
# SERIES

## *Leader's Guide*

### Carol J. Ruvolo

P U B L I S H I N G
P.O. BOX 817 • PHILLIPSBURG • NEW JERSEY 08865-0817

Unless otherwise indicated, Scripture quotations are from the New American Standard Bible. Copyright by the Lockman Foundation 1960, 1962, 1963, 1968, 1971, 1973, 1975, 1977.

Printed in the United States of America

Composition by Colophon Typesetting

ISBN 0-87552-628-4

# CONTENTS

CHAPTER 1
From Our Hearts to Yours
1

CHAPTER 2
Wanted: A Few Gifted Leaders
2

CHAPTER 3
A Little Light on the Series
7

CHAPTER 4
I Am Their Leader—Which Way Did They Go?
16

CHAPTER 5
A Little Help from Some Friends
24

NOTES
27

# From Our Hearts to Yours

P&R Publishing and I want to thank you for choosing the Light for Your Path Series for your women's Bible study. We appreciate your commitment to building up the body of Christ through serious Bible study. We pray that the series will encourage all of you to grow in God's grace and live out your transformation in Jesus Christ.

We have worked hard to make this series beneficial to women at all levels of Christian maturity and have developed this *Leaders' Guide* to help *you,* their leader, help *them* get the most from their study. As you read through the guide, you will see that it is indeed a *guide,* not an answer book or a detailed procedure manual. The studies in the Light for Your Path Series encourage women to think carefully about the material presented and complete the study exercises *in their own words.* We believe we can best encourage *you,* their leader, to encourage *them* to do that by *not* giving you "suggested answers."

Instead, we offer you this guide to use a lot or a little, depending on your background and experience in leading Bible study groups. It contains some important reminders for teachers, a description of the Light for Your Path Series, a few suggestions for leading your group, and a list of other helpful resources. Use it prayerfully, and ask the Holy Spirit to guide your implementation of its counsel.

May the God who has called you to minister in His service richly bless your efforts on His behalf!

# 2

# Wanted: A Few Gifted Leaders

Not everyone is a leader. And that's good because if all people were leaders, they would have nothing to do! The apostle Paul tells us in Romans 12 that whether we lead or follow in ministry depends, in large part, on our spiritual giftedness. Some gifts specifically equip leaders to lead, and others specifically equip followers to follow. However, none of us fits exclusively into either category. We all lead some people while following others.

"Leadership," then, is never absolute. It is largely a matter of degree. That is clearly demonstrated in the case of women who have been gifted and called to positions of leadership in the church. They have been called not to lead the church in general, nor men in particular, but *other women* in the church while following the ordained *men* who lead the church and who, in turn, follow God.

If you are reading this guide, chances are very good that you are one of those women and that your leadership gifts lie in the area of teaching. If you have been so gifted, you have also been greatly blessed. You stand as a vital link between God and His people as you draw on the gifts He has given you to teach His people His truths and to encourage them to apply them. Your gifts thoroughly equip you to greatly influence those you teach. Daniel 12:3 describes *you* when it says, "And those who have insight will shine brightly like the brightness of the expanse of heaven, and those who lead the many to righteousness, like the stars forever and ever."

Those who have been gifted to teach usually are deeply committed to Christian ministry. Paul described his call as a "compulsion" (1 Corinthians 9:16). Ezra "set his heart to study the law of the LORD, and to practice it, and to teach His statutes and ordinances in Israel" (Ezra 7:10). If you have been gifted to teach, you probably identify with those statements. You teach because you can't not teach. You don't give up easily, and you work hard to teach well. You do this because you feel the weight of the responsibility God has called you to bear.

Part of that responsibility involves allowing Scripture to remind you, from time to time, of God's expectations and gracious enabling. As you and I join together (teacher-writer with teacher-leader) to embark on this Light for Your Path study, let's take a moment to be reminded of some basics.

## Basic Requirements

*Control Your Tongue.* We teachers are expected to control our tongues. James 3:1–2 says, "Let not many of you become teachers, my brethren, knowing that as such we shall incur a stricter judgment. For we all stumble in many ways. If anyone does not stumble in what he says, he is a perfect man, able to bridle the whole body as well." We teachers, who minister with our tongues, run the risk of stumbling in what we say. We must prepare our lessons carefully and deliver them thoughtfully so that we will not be guilty of leading our students away from the truth instead of toward it.

As teachers, we will incur a stricter judgment because we influence the way our students think and live. Thus, we become responsible not only for our own behavior but, to a significant degree, for the behavior of our students as well. We must not forget that our ministry has a ripple effect that increases our accountability before God.

*Teach Out of Love.* We must be motivated by love. First Timothy 1:5–7 says, "The goal of our instruction is love from a pure heart and a good conscience and a sincere faith. For some men, straying from these things, have turned aside to fruitless discussion, wanting to be teachers of the Law, even though they do not understand either what they are saying or the matters about which they make confident assertions." One of the best ways to teach our students to love is to teach them lovingly.

First Corinthians 13:5 tells us that love "does not seek its own." Instead it seeks what is best for the one loved. That means working hard to help our students understand and apply God's truth. In order to do that, we must be patient with them and kind to them. We must not exalt ourselves by teaching arrogantly or bragging about our position. We must not be easily provoked or hold grudges. We must pursue righteousness and love truth. And we must persevere in hope. We must also seek to protect our students from self-appointed "teachers" who would lead them astray by making confident assertions about things they don't understand.

This kind of love cannot be lived out in one or two hours a week. It is a full-time job that extends beyond the classroom. As teachers of love who are motivated by love, we are always "on call."

**Handle the Word Accurately.** Second Timothy 2:15 says, "Be diligent to present yourself approved to God as a workman who does not need to be ashamed, handling accurately the word of truth." The only way to face our stricter judgment and to instruct our students in love is to handle Scripture accurately. Effective teachers study diligently. That means committing the necessary time and energy to understanding the material and explaining it well. It means being willing to "work overtime," seeking answers to puzzling questions and refusing to settle for superficiality. It means studying the Bible systematically and deliberately in our own private study and in submission to other God-appointed teachers.

**Practice What You Teach.** Paul asks in Romans 2:21–23, "You, therefore, who teach another, do you not teach yourself? You who preach that one should not steal, do you steal? You who say that one should not commit adultery, do you commit adultery? You who abhor idols, do you rob temples? You who boast in the Law, through your breaking the Law, do you dishonor God?"

I don't mind telling you that some of the most difficult times in my own life have been those in which God has required me to *apply* something I have taught. But I hasten to add that they have also been times of great blessing. Not only does God glorify Himself in our obedience, but He also uses the humbling process of our learning obedience to deepen our compassion for the people we teach.

Second Timothy 2:21–26 reminds us that teachers who desire to be vessels of honor, sanctified and useful to the Master, must apply what they teach by fleeing from youthful lusts, and pursuing "righteousness, faith, love and peace, with those who call on the Lord from a pure heart." They must "refuse foolish and ignorant speculations, knowing that they produce quarrels," and must "not be quarrelsome, but be kind to all, able to teach, patient when wronged, with gentleness correcting those who are in opposition." Our actions almost always communicate more loudly than our words. When our actions reinforce our words by consistently reflecting them, we will have the greatest impact on our students.

**Rely on God's Power.** Paul wrote to the Philippians, "Work out your salvation with fear and trembling; for it is God who is at work in you, both to will and to work for His good pleasure" (2:12–13). He applied this principle in his own ministry. "But by the grace of God I am what I am, and His grace toward me did not prove vain; but I labored even more than all of them, yet not I, but the grace of God with me" (1 Corinthians 15:10).

If this principle was true in Paul's ministry, it is certainly true in ours. We simply cannot minister in our own strength. We must draw our confidence and adequacy wholly from God. "And such confidence we have through Christ toward God. Not that we are adequate in ourselves to consider anything as coming from ourselves, but our adequacy is from God" (2 Corinthians 3:4–5).

## A Joint Venture

Now that we have taken the time to be reminded of some things, let's spend a few minutes looking at what is ahead of us. We are embarking on a joint venture intended to build up the body of Christ. Many people have already contributed to the venture. I have written the studies, my pastor and elders have read and critiqued them, and I have revised them. The women of my church have worked through several of the drafts and made suggestions. And I revised them again. A group of gifted, creative, and hard-working saints at P&R Publishing have edited them (more revision!), designed them, and made them available to the Christian community. All of this was done before you ever saw them, and with God's ongoing blessing, will continue as more studies are prepared.

But all that work represents only the beginning of the venture. Now that these studies are in your hands, the rest is up to you. A series of Bible studies sitting on bookstore shelves or on your desk does not build up the body of Christ. They must be used. They must be studied and applied.

You, the leader of a women's Bible study, occupy the pivotal position in the rest of the venture. God has called you to lead a group of women toward understanding and applying the biblical truths presented in the Light for Your Path Series. It may seem like a daunting task. But God will fully equip you for every good work (2 Timothy 3:16–17) and "make all grace abound to you, that always having all sufficiency in everything, you may have an abundance for every good deed" (2 Corinthians 9:8).

As you lead other women, impress upon them *their* role in the venture. Each of them has been uniquely gifted for ministry and should view Bible study as part of her equipping to exercise her gifts. When all the members of the body of Christ work together, united in spirit and intent on one purpose, the body as a whole is strengthened and built up. But it is seriously weakened when renegade members don their "Lone Ranger" costumes and ride off into the sunset.

As you lead, I will be praying for you and asking the Lord to finish the work He has begun in the Light for Your Path Series. The remaining chapters in this guide describe the series and offer some practical suggestions for using it in your group. If I can be of any further assistance to you, I would be delighted to hear from you. Please feel free to contact me through P&R Publishing.

CHAPTER

# 3

# A Little Light on the Series

*This chapter is an expansion of the preface included in each Light for Your Path study.[1] It contains everything your students will read in that preface plus additional material about the series that will help you lead the studies more effectively.*

## The Purpose

"Man's chief end is to glorify God and to enjoy Him forever," declares one of Christianity's well-known catechisms.[2] Most of the Christians I know wouldn't dream of disputing that statement. But precious few actually live it out.

*Why not?* I have often wondered. If they have been transformed by regeneration in Jesus Christ (2 Corinthians 5:17; Romans 6:14, 17–18) and have everything they need to glorify God and enjoy Him forever (2 Corinthians 9:8), why don't they do it? Years of thinking (it takes me a while) have produced only two reasonable answers: (1) Those Christians know very little of the truth contained in God's Word, and/or (2) they have never learned how to apply the scriptural truth they do know in everyday life.

The studies in the Light for Your Path Series were written to help change that. Their purpose is to teach women how to glorify God and enjoy Him forever by living out their transformation in Jesus Christ. The studies reflect my own commitment to the Bible as the infallible, inerrant, authoritative, and entirely sufficient Word of God to humanity, and my belief that Reformed theology is the clearest and most accurate statement of biblical truth. This purpose and commitment should be repeatedly emphasized as you work through each study with your students.

## Types of Studies

The series begins with two foundational studies, *A Book Like No Other: What's So Special About the Bible* (six lessons) and *Turning On the Light: Discovering the Riches of God's Word* (seven lessons). These two studies lay the essential foundation for the remaining studies by presenting the unique character of God's revelation and an effective approach to studying it. If your Sunday school or Bible study groups are structured in thirteen-week quarters, I recommend combining these two studies in your first quarter of study.

The remaining studies in the Light for Your Path Series each contain thirteen lessons and fall into two categories. "Light" studies cover particular books of the Bible and concentrate on discovering the meaning and appropriate applications of the text under consideration. You will recognize them by their subtitles, which always begin with the words *Light from*.

"Focus" studies seek to bring the whole counsel of God to bear on specific topics, such as salvation, prayer, relationships, or righteousness, in order to develop godly understanding, motivation, and behavior regarding the topic under discussion. You will also recognize them by their subtitles, which begin with the words *Focus on*.

I recommend using both types of studies in your group—perhaps alternating them—to provide your students with a balanced "Bible study diet" that will richly nourish them and encourage Christian growth. "Light" studies provide their necessary grounding in the Word of God while "Focus" studies sharpen their ability to relate scriptural truth to daily life.

## Dangers: Context Abuse and Selective Proof Texting

Both types of Bible studies present challenges to you as their leader. Topical studies, because they deal with Scripture passages scattered throughout the Bible, are particularly prone to *context abuse* and *selective proof texting.*

*Context abuse* occurs when a verse or passage is isolated from its surroundings to support a point not intended by its author. For example, how many times have you heard Matthew 7:1 ("Do not judge lest you be judged") used to support the idea that Christians should never confront, correct, or discipline others regarding sin? Standing alone, this verse might seem to say that. But when studied in context, it takes on a very different meaning.

*Selective proof texting* occurs when only those verses seeming to support a particular view are cited, while those seeming to refute that view are ignored. You may have heard selective proof texting in discussions about whether Christians can lose their salvation. Those who say salvation can be lost are quick to cite Galatians 5:4; Hebrews 6:4–5; 10:26–27; and 2 Peter 3:17 but rarely mention John 10:27–30 or Romans 8:31–39. Those who rightly emphasize our security in Christ have sometimes neglected biblical warnings about falling away. It's no wonder people say, "You can prove anything you want from the Bible."

Topical studies require you to follow the example of the noble Bereans in Acts 17 by "examining the Scriptures daily, to see whether these things [are] so" (v. 11). The best way to do this is by (1) conscientiously checking the context of isolated verses and (2) identifying what else the Bible says about the subject you are studying.

**Check the context.** The Bible was originally written in sentences and paragraphs without the chapter and verse designations that were later added to help readers find passages. Remembering this will help you put isolated verses back into their proper context.

Let's practice by checking the context of Matthew 7:1. First, see if the referenced verse contains one or more *complete sentences*. (Remember, a complete sentence contains a subject and a verb, begins with a capital letter, and ends with a period, question mark, or exclamation point.) So far, so good. Matthew 7:1 is a complete sentence. If the text you are examining includes any incomplete sentences, back up and/or read further to find what is missing.

Then read your text in the context of the *full* sentence(s) you have found.

Next, let's look for the *paragraph* containing Matthew 7:1. Some Bibles are actually formatted in standard indented paragraphs, while others use bold type or a figure (such as ¶) to mark the beginning of a new paragraph. Check the introductory material in your Bible if necessary, and then find the beginning and end of the paragraph in which Matthew 7:1 occurs.

Found it? It begins in Matthew 7:1 and runs through the end of verse 5. Now read the entire paragraph, and ask yourself what subject is being discussed and how Matthew 7:1 relates to that subject. If you have time, read the surrounding paragraphs to get an even broader idea of the context. Once you have done this, I think you will see that this verse does not prohibit evaluation of each other's behavior according to the standard of Scripture. Instead, it warns us not to do that *before* we have applied the same standard to *ourselves*.

Your preparation to lead your group should include a "routine background check" of the context of verses used to support points in the lesson material. I have made a valiant effort to avoid abusing the context of the verses I have cited in my topical studies. My pastor has come alongside me to help in that endeavor, as have my elders and my publisher, but none of us is infallible. If you find an abuse of context in any of these studies, please let me know.[3]

**Identifying What Else Scripture Says on the Subject.** There are several ways you can do this. The easiest is checking the cross-references in your Bible. These will direct you to other verses that discuss the same words or ideas.

You should also own and know how to use an *exhaustive concordance*. This invaluable reference tool lists, alphabetically, every word found in the Bible, followed by the verses in which each word appears. Many exhaustive concordances incorporate a numbering system that allows you to identify and define the original Hebrew and Greek words behind the English words you are looking up. A topical Bible such as *Nave's* can also be very helpful because it lists references by topics, allowing you to access verses that may discuss the same idea in different words.

Of course, the best way to identify what else Scripture has to say on a particular subject is to become increasingly familiar with the Bible as a whole. A good systematic reading program will help you do this. Most reading schedules take you "through the Bible in a year," but the time period is not that important. What *is* important is reading the entire Bible on a regular basis so that you become familiar with its overall message.

A good Scripture memorization program also helps you to remember what the Bible as a whole says on a topic. Recalling, for example, that Scripture instructs us to exhort, reprove, rebuke, correct, or discipline each other (as in Proverbs 27:5; 28:23; Matthew 7:6; 18:15–20; 1 Corinthians 6:1–11; Galatians 6:1–5) will help you to see that Matthew 7:1 does not forbid such forms of judging. Scripture never contradicts itself.

## One More Danger: Application Neglect

Book studies are less susceptible to context abuse and selective proof texting, but seem to be more prone to *application neglect*. Your study group may get so wrapped up in interpreting the text that they forget to apply what they have learned. To help them guard against this tendency, pay particular attention to the application questions when you are working through the "Light" studies in this series.

## What Makes These Studies Distinct

Even though "Light" studies and "Focus" studies differ in their approach to discovering biblical truth, they are very similar in their structure and format. Both contain several pages of written lesson material followed by exercises. I think you will find the exercises, in particular, significantly different from those you have encountered in other women's Bible studies. The exercises are distinct in a number of ways.

First of all, they have been designed to nurture and challenge women at varying levels of spiritual maturity. The Light for Your Path Series does not target "new believers" or "mature believers" or "middle-aged believers." Rather, it targets all believers. I have tried to write exercises that will encourage women of all levels of maturity to study together in the same group because I believe such a mix benefits everyone. New believers gain valuable insights from women who have been studying the Bible for years, and mature believers are refreshed and encouraged by close encounters with fresh faith.

Second, the exercises are structured as "essay" assignments that require women to *think about* what they have studied and express it *in their own words.* Answering questions in this manner helps women distinguish what they truly understand from the nice-sounding-but-meaningless catch phrases that are so popular in Christian circles.

Third, the exercises stimulate advancement through various levels of learning. Dennis H. Dirks, in *Christian Education: Foundations for the Future,* describes and defines five levels of learning in Christian education:

(1) knowledge—the essential foundation of biblical facts. For example: Salvation is wholly of God's grace.

(2) understanding—the ability to express biblical concepts in terms that have personal meaning. For example: My salvation is wholly God's doing; I did nothing to save myself.

(3) application—the ability to put truth into practice, that is, to address issues of life in ways that are consistent with Scripture. For example: One way I can put the interests of others ahead of my own is to cook a nice dinner for my husband on a night when he doesn't feel like going out—even though I am tired and would *love* to go out.

(4) synthesis—the ability to bring biblical concepts together so that new insights are gained. For example: Relating the *concept* of self-sacrifice to the *principle* of forgiveness produces a deeper understanding of the *meaning* of forgiveness.

(5) evaluation—the ability to determine the value of a particular decision, action, idea, or attitude in light of biblical standards. For example, evaluating the biblical validity of several possible responses to various social issues such as civil disobedience, legalizing abortion, and discharging homosexuals from the military.[4]

The first two levels of learning listed above form an essential foundation for the final three. But standing alone, they will not support a dynamic Christian witness that glorifies God. Tragically, a great deal of teaching in the church today fails to rise above the first level. The Light for Your Path Series seeks to provide a remedy for this situation by imparting essential level-1 knowledge in the written lesson material, and then pulling women into levels 2 through 5 in the exercises.

## Three Kinds of Exercises

The exercises are broken into three sections: *Review, application,* and *digging deeper.* The preface in each study explains these exercises to your students. Take time to make sure they understand them.

The *review* exercises help women determine how well they have understood the lesson material by giving them an opportunity to express the key points in their own words (level-2 learning.) The *application* exercises encourage them to put their understanding of the lesson material to work in daily life (level-3 learning). And the *digging deeper* exercises challenge them to pursue further study in certain key areas while emphasizing synthesis and evaluation (levels 4 and 5).

The answers to the *review* exercises can be found in the lesson material itself but should not be simply copied from the text. Encourage your students to put these ideas into their own words. When they can do this, they know they *understand* what they have read. If they are having trouble doing this, remind them of a suggestion offered in the preface, which is to ask, "How would I explain this idea to someone if I didn't have the book with me?"

The *application* exercises ask your students to apply certain elements of the lesson material to their personal situations. Remind the women to consider their time constraints when answering these questions. Many will not have time to answer more than one question well. Encourage them to pray over the questions and ask the Lord to show them which one(s) *He* wants them to work on. Applications of biblical truth should take a significant amount of time and thought. Genuine applications are never quick or easy, and beneficial applications are always constructed in specific terms rather than in vague generalities.

For example, let's say you are applying the truths found in Philippians 2:3–4 concerning regarding others as more important than yourself by putting their interests ahead of your own. The following "application" is a vague generality: "I need to be more helpful and kind to those around me." A specific application would look more like this: "I will call my daughter this morning (who lives in a sorority house on the local college campus) and cheerfully offer to edit her term paper while she studies for her final exams. If she accepts my offer, I will do my Saturday chores on Friday, leaving Saturday free to help her."

Do you see the difference? A specific application answers the questions:

- Who? (my daughter)
- What? (call and volunteer to edit her paper; rearrange my chores)
- When? (call this morning; edit the paper Saturday; do the chores on Friday)
- Where? (call from my living room; edit the paper at home or in her room, whichever is more convenient for her)
- How? (cheerfully)

A vague generality does not answer these questions. Encourage your students to make specific applications in the areas of their thinking, their attitudes, and/or their behavior. And help them understand that vague generalities do not help them grow in their faith and do not glorify God.[5]

*Digging deeper* exercises usually require a significant amount of time and effort to complete. They are designed to challenge mature Christians who are eager for more advanced study. However, new Christians should be encouraged to read them and work on any that pique their interest. The Holy Spirit may well be pleased to use one or more of these meaty exercises to stimulate growth in *any* believer. Regardless of our maturity level, we all grow by stretching beyond where we are right now, and working on one or more of these exercises may help *any* of your students do that.

(Below I'll say more about how to handle these different types of exercises during your class time.)

Urge your students to resist the temptation to compete with each other. The purpose of any Bible study (and these in particular) is to stimulate growth in faith and life by learning and applying God's truth—not to fill up a study book with impressive answers. Remind the women frequently that if they learn and apply *one element* of God's truth in each lesson, they are consistently moving beyond where they were when they began, and in doing so, are accomplishing what Bible study is all about.

CHAPTER 4

# I Am Their Leader— Which Way Did They Go?

If you have been leading women's Bible studies for any length of time, you probably smiled when you read that heading. You've been there. I smiled when I wrote it because I've been there too. Every leader, at one time or another, experiences that queasy feeling of helpless panic when he or she suddenly realizes, "I've lost 'em!" The suggestions below should decrease the frequency of those leader-panic attacks, though I'm sure they won't eliminate them.

The Light for Your Path Series may require you to take a slightly different approach to leadership. I recommend that you carefully read through this chapter and prayerfully determine which of these suggestions are most appropriate for your particular group. If you would like additional input or counsel, please feel free to contact me personally through P&R Publishing.

## Getting Organized

Leading your Light for Your Path study begins with *planning*. If you have not used this material before, read this guide and then work through at least one of the studies on your own or with a trusted friend. After doing that, if you believe the women in your church will benefit from the series, work with your Women In the Church council (or other women's leadership group) to prepare a proposal to submit to your church leaders (the session of elders, or church board) for approval. Be prepared to appear before your leaders to answer their questions about the series if necessary.

In developing a coherent proposal to submit to your church leaders, you will need to consider, in addition to the strengths and benefits of the series, such things as the following:

***Class Size.*** You may want to suggest two or more classes that meet at different times if you need to accommodate a large number of women. Be realistic about your own abilities and time constraints, and seek out other teacher-leaders who are willing to help you if necessary.

***Class Makeup.*** Will you limit the study to women who attend your church? Will you invite other churches in the community to participate? Will you open your study to the community at large? In considering this issue, be aware that the Light for Your Path Series was not intended as an evangelistic tool although God could certainly be pleased to use it for that purpose.

Be aware also, that opening your class to other Christians in your community may be a good way of introducing them to the great truths of Reformed theology. A few of the most committed students in my classes attend "non-Reformed" churches. If you suggest this, however, be sure you or someone else in your group is familiar enough with Reformed doctrines to explain them to the women who will undoubtedly ask questions.

***Time and Place.*** When and where will you meet? You might want to conduct an informal survey of the women in your church to discover the best times of day and location for your class. I was very surprised to discover that the majority of the women in my church preferred meeting at noon. Some groups enjoy meeting in someone's home, while others opt for the more studious atmosphere of a church classroom.

***Child Care.*** Will you provide a nursery? If you do, how will you staff it? Can your church afford to hire a nursery attendant? Do you have teenagers in your church who are available and willing to minister to student-moms in this way? I recommend that you *not* rotate women in the study through the nursery because it breaks the continuity of the study for them.

If you cannot provide a nursery, I would caution you *against* encouraging women to bring their children with them to the study. Most women find it very difficult to concentrate on serious Bible study when their children are in the room, and other women in the group may also find them distracting. You will benefit your students greatly by guarding this brief time of focused study as completely as you can, even though you may have to make an occasional exception.

**Sequence of Studies.** I recommend beginning with *A Book Like No Other* and *Turning On the Light* to lay a firm foundation for the remaining studies. Once your group has digested these two, feel free to choose studies from those currently available that will meet the needs of your particular group. Seek to maintain a balance of book and topical studies if at all possible.

## Getting the Word Out

After receiving approval from your church leaders, you will need to determine the start and end dates for your study. Keep in mind that you may structure your class in a thirteen- or fourteen-week format. Each study in the Light for Your Path Series contains thirteen lessons. (*A Book Like No Other* and *Turning On the Light* contain thirteen lessons when combined.) Therefore, you may plan to complete one lesson each week, or you may use your first class meeting for an introductory lesson.

Once you have decided upon the dates for your class, prepare an information sheet for distribution to your target group (your church, other churches, and/or the community at large). Include the following information:

- the name of the series,
- the name of the study you are leading,
- the dates, times, and meeting place of the class,
- your name and phone number,
- a brief description of the class,

– an idea of what will be expected from the students,

– a date by which interested women may contact you.

Distribute these sheets several weeks before your class is scheduled to begin. Include a request for interested women to contact you before the specified date.

## Getting Started

While you are collecting responses, begin working on your introductory material. If you have chosen a thirteen-week format, prepare an assignment sheet instructing your students how to prepare for the first class meeting. Plan on giving this sheet to them along with their books at least two weeks before the first class meeting. If you chose a fourteen-week format, begin preparing your introductory lesson.

Each study in the Light for Your Path Series contains introductory material that should be covered before lesson 1 is prepared. Plan on presenting it in your introductory lesson or designating it as "required reading" in your assignment sheet. I also recommend that you reiterate the following information (from the preface of each Light for Your Path study) regarding their preparation for study:

> Bible study is a serious task that involves a significant investment of time and energy. Preparing yourself to study effectively will help you reap the greatest benefit from that investment. Study when you are well rested and alert. Try to find a time and place that is quiet, free of distractions, and conducive to concentration. Use a loose-leaf or spiral notebook to take notes on what you read and to do the exercises in this study. You may also want to develop a simple filing system so that you can refer to these notes in later studies.
>
> Approach Bible study as you would any task that requires thought and effort to do well. Don't be surprised if it challenges you and stretches your thinking. Expect it to be difficult at times but extremely rewarding.

Always begin your study with prayer. Ask the Lord to reveal sin in your life that needs to be confessed and cleansed, to help you concentrate on His truths, and to illumine your mind with understanding of what He has written. End your study with a prayer for opportunities to apply what you have learned and wisdom to recognize those opportunities when they occur.

As soon as you know how many women will be attending your class, order your books. Check with your local bookstore or contact P&R Direct (1-800-631-0094) to order, and be sure to allow plenty of time for shipping. You may want to order two or three extra books for women who show up at the last minute with a contrite, "Oh, was I supposed to call you?"

### Lead On: Using the Lesson Material

The final step in leading your study is, of course, *leading it*. How you do that is largely up to you and the Holy Spirit, but I would like to share my preferences for dealing with the rather unusual format of these studies.

First of all, I have found it largely unnecessary to lecture on the written material since the review exercises cover the material adequately. When the women know their class time will be built around an extensive discussion of the exercises, they tend to prepare more thoroughly.

Some of the application exercises are very personal and may not lend themselves to class discussion. Assure the women that they will not be pressured to share anything they would rather keep private. But emphasize how important it is for them to work through the application exercises regardless of whether they share them.

Since most of the digging deeper exercises are quite involved, you should not expect yourself or anyone else to complete all of them. I have several suggestions regarding how you might approach them and would love to hear from you if you can think of any others.

The first (and easiest) way to deal with these questions is *not* to deal with them—at least during your class time. If they seem overwhelming to you or the majority of your women, simply tell your class to look them over and work individually on any they find appealing. Offer your assistance if you are comfortable doing so, or point them toward their pastor, an elder, or other church leaders for help.

The second option is "one step up" from the first but requires little extra effort on your part. During your preparation, examine the digging deeper exercises and prepare a "plan of attack" for working on each one. Then reserve the last five minutes of your class period to offer your plan of attack for anyone who would like to pursue the exercises on her own. Again offer your assistance or be prepared to guide interested women to other sources of help.

The next three options will work best in groups containing several mature women who really like to study. These options should not be attempted unless you know your group fairly well. First, you may ask for volunteers to prepare one (or more) of the digging deeper exercises for presentation to the class each week. This is a particularly good option if you have mature women in your class with teaching gifts. It spreads out the burden and gives them an opportunity to teach. If you choose this option, give the women several weeks to prepare if at all possible.

Or, you may instruct your students to work independently on these exercises (all of them or a few selected ones) throughout the entire semester and then gather for one final class period to discuss them all. (You can make this a "celebration of completion" by structuring this class around a "pot-providence" brunch and handing out diplomas.)

Or, you may structure your study on two meetings per week instead of one. The first meeting would include the entire class and involve discussion of the review and application exercises, while the second meeting would include only those women interested in discussing the digging deeper exercises. This option requires a formidable amount of work for the leader and should be undertaken, in my opinion, by a team of teacher-leaders rather than an individual.

Finally, if your group is large and organized as a lecture time followed by small group discussion, you may want to consider devoting your lecture material to one or more of the digging deeper questions. The review and application questions could then be discussed in the small groups.

— — —

The Light for Your Path Series, because of its distinctive format, may well challenge and stretch your creative teaching "instincts." I encourage you to teach this material as creatively as you can without sacrificing orthodoxy and to share with me any effective approaches you come up with.

## Teaching Tips

Here are a few additional teaching tips with which you may already be familiar. I offer them as a reminder.

1. Begin and end your class periods on time. Many women live on tight schedules and greatly appreciate this courtesy.

2. Begin your class time with prayer. Acknowledge your dependence on the Holy Spirit's guidance, and focus everyone's attention on your purpose for gathering.

3. Encourage everyone to participate. You may have to ask a quiet woman a specific question or suggest, "Let's hear from someone who hasn't spoken up yet."

4. Don't be afraid to say "I don't know." If a question comes up that you can't answer, query the class to see if anyone else can. If not, offer to dig out the answer during the week, or ask if someone else would enjoy taking up that challenge.

5. Apportion your time to cover the material adequately each week. I allot approximately two-thirds of my class time to the review exercises and the remaining one-third to discussion of the application and digging deeper exercises.

6. Avoid rabbit trails. Offer to discuss side issues after class, or schedule time to meet with "the rabbit" later in the week.

7. Don't let silences unnerve you. Give your students time to think about their comments. If silence persists, back up and rephrase.

8. Stress biblical support for comments. This is, without a doubt, the best way to handle "off the wall" statements. One of the finest teachers I know is fond of asking (with a smile), "You got a verse for that?" I always make it a point to tell my classes, "Feel free to disagree with anything I say, as long as you can support your argument biblically." I also tell them that they are free to ask me for biblical support for any of my statements.

9. Be as available as you can to your students. If at all possible, give them your home phone number and times when you are free to take their calls.

10. Finally, remember to nourish yourself. Howard Hendricks said it well: "If you stop growing today, you stop teaching tomorrow. . . . You cannot communicate out of a vacuum. You cannot impart what you do not possess. If you don't know it—truly know it—you can't give it."[6]

# 5
# A Little Help from Some Friends

The following list of resources represents only a fraction of the fine reference works available today for teacher-leaders and is offered as an aid in building your personal library:

1. Bible translations: Have several on hand for use in your study. The most accurate and reliable translations are the *New King James Version, New American Standard Bible,* and the *New International Version.* If you use Bible paraphrases in your study, consider them commentaries, not translations. In my opinion, the best study Bible on the market today is the *New Geneva Study Bible* published by Nelson.

2. Concordances: You should own at least one exhaustive concordance. Choose the one that corresponds to the Bible translation you use most often.

3. *Nave's Topical Bible* allows you to research by topic rather than by words.

4. A chronological Bible is an interesting reference tool that arranges the books of the Bible in chronological rather than the traditional order.

5. *The Treasury of Scripture Knowledge,* by R. A. Torrey, is an exhaustive collection of cross references.

6. *Nelson's Complete Book of Bible Maps and Charts* is a veritable treasure-trove of maps and charts you can copy to use in your classes.

7. An expository dictionary of Bible words (such as *Vine's*) used in conjunction with your exhaustive concordance will allow you to research Hebrew and Greek words.

8. Howard Hendricks's *Teaching to Change Lives* will provide delightful assistance in improving your teaching skills.

9. An inexpensive volume of maps for quick reference is G. Ernest Wright and Floyd V. Filson's *Westminster Historical Maps of Bible Lands.*

10. Excellent Bible atlases:

    − Carl G. Rasmussen, *Zondervan NIV Atlas of the Bible*
    − Charles F. Pfeiffer, *Baker's Bible Atlas*
    − Herbert G. May, ed., *Oxford Bible Atlas*

11. Excellent Bible dictionaries:

    − *The New International Dictionary of the Bible* (edited by J. D. Douglas and Merrill C. Tenney)
    − *The New Unger's Bible Dictionary* (edited by Merrill F. Unger)
    − *The New Bible Dictionary* (edited by J. D. Douglas)

12. A few recommended theologians and commentators:

    − John Calvin
    − Louis Berkhof
    − B. B. Warfield
    − J. Gresham Machen
    − D. Martyn Lloyd-Jones

- John Murray
- William Hendriksen/Simon J. Kistemaker
- R. C. Sproul
- James Montgomery Boice
- A. W. Pink
- James I. Packer
- Jay E. Adams
- Edmund P. Clowney

# Notes

1. Much of this material is also included in the preface to my Faith at Work series on the book of James, published by Deo Volente.

2. *The Shorter Catechism with Scripture Proofs* (Carlisle, Pa.: Banner of Truth, n.d.), 1.

3. See lessons 3 and 4 of *Turning On the Light* for more information about the importance of context.

4. Dennis H. Dirks, "The Teacher: Facilitator for Change," in *Christian Education: Foundations for the Future,* ed. Robert E. Clark, Lin Johnson, and Allyn K. Sloat, (Chicago: Moody Press, 1991), 147–48; I have numbered and amplified these descriptions slightly.

5. See lesson 6 of *Turning On the Light* for more information about application.

6. Howard G. Hendricks, *Teaching to Change Lives* (Portland, Ore.: Multnomah, 1987), 27.